10/98

20.40

Put on Some Antlers and Walk Like a

moose

How Scientists Find, Follow, and Study Wild Animals

APRIL PULLEY SAYRE

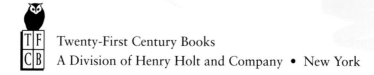

Twenty-First Century Books
A Division of Henry Holt and Company • New York

ACKNOWLEDGMENTS

Special thanks go to the many people who helped in gathering information and reviewing facts for this book. They include: Jeff Sayre, my husband and wetland-slogging compatriot; Sarah Anderson, Department of Science, St. Ann's School, Brooklyn, New York; Dr. G. A. Bubenik, Department of Zoology, University of Guelph, Ontario; Christine Taafe of the Vector Biology Laboratory at Notre Dame; Dr. David Lodge of the Department of Biological Sciences at Notre Dame; Dr. Patricia Wright of the Department of Biological Anthropology, SUNY at Stony Brook; Sy Montgomery; Phoebe Lewan; and two anonymous owl banders at Whitefish Point Bird Observatory, Michigan.

———

Twenty-First Century Books
A Division of Henry Holt and Company, Inc.
115 West 18th Street
New York, NY 10011

Henry Holt® and colophon are trademarks of
Henry Holt and Company, Inc.
Publishers since 1866

Library of Congress Cataloging-in-Publication Data
Sayre, April Pulley.
Put on some antlers and walk like a moose: how scientists find,
follow, and study wild animals / by April Pulley Sayre.
p.   cm.
Includes bibliographical references (p.) and index.
Summary: Describes the work of field scientists who study animals in their natural habitats,
discussing the challenges of finding the animals, tracking them, and recording data about them.
ISBN 0-8050-5182-1
1. Zoology—Research—Juvenile literature. 2. Zoology—Field work—Juvenile literature.
3. Nature study—Juvenile literature. [1. Zoologists. 2. Zoology.] I. Title.
QL51S385 1997
590′.7′23—dc21   97-8072
                                                                           CIP
                                                                           AC

DESIGNED BY KELLY SOONG

Printed in the United States of America
All first editions are printed on acid-free paper ∞.

1 3 5 7 9 10 8 6 4 2

Photo credits appear on page 79.

CONTENTS

INTRODUCTION

Last May, at midnight under a starry sky, I stood hip deep in mud in a Michigan wetland. That's the kind of thing you do if you're a scientist, or in my case, a science writer in pursuit of a particular animal. Scientists have been known to hang from ropes, crouch in caves, dive into rivers, and growl like gorillas, in order to study animals. There was even a scientist, Dr. Anthony Bubenik, who wore a moose head, complete with antlers, just to attract moose.

Bubenik was a biologist for the Ontario Ministry of Natural Resources and a world-renowned expert on antlers. One of his famous experiments, which was filmed by his wife, Marie, concerned the effect of antler size. First, Bubenik put small antlers on the moose head he was wearing. A wild moose saw him and took little notice. Next, he put on a huge pair of antlers, and the same moose ran away. Finally, he put on a pair of antlers that was the same size as the other moose's antlers and the moose charged. Bubenik had to abandon his moose costume and quickly run for cover!

Bubenik's experiment—concise, creative, maybe a little crazy—was on my mind that night when I stood in Michigan mud. I was thinking about what lengths a scientist will go to in order to study an animal. A few yards from me, Richard Urbanek, a biologist for Seney National Wildlife Refuge, was tapping two pebbles together. *Clack, clack . . . clack, clack, clack.* For the better part of an hour, he made the crisp, repetitive noise over and over until it was branded into my brain. Fortunately, despite the chilly air and cold water, I stayed warm and dry, wearing chest waders—the rubber pants and boots fishermen wear. But the reason we were there, the reason this scientist was tapping pebbles together, remained hidden in the low, matted plants.

Clack, clack . . . clack, clack, clack. Just when I thought the pebble tapping would make me scream, the animal replied. *Clack, clack . . . clack, clack, clack*, it called. The noise was loud . . . and unbelievably close. It sounded exactly like the tapping of pebbles, even though the animal made the noise with its throat.

Clacking back and forth, Urbanek and the animal continued their "conversation" for another forty-five minutes. Then, finally, out walked a tiny bird, no more than 7 inches (18 centimeters) long. It was the elusive marsh bird we sought: the yellow rail.

In a swift, smooth movement, Urbanek netted the rail. He extracted it from the net and banded it, clamping a numbered metal bracelet around the bird's leg. Then he set the rail loose. The job done, we slogged back to the truck.

By capturing and banding yellow rails, Urbanek can identify and study them individually. When a bird is recaptured, he can check the numbers on its

Banding helps Richard Urbanek (left) to keep track of the yellow rail population at Seney National Wildlife Refuge.

band to see which individual bird it is. Comparing this number with banding records from previous years can reveal how old the bird is and how many years it has returned to the place where it was captured. The total number of birds banded year to year can give Urbanek an indication of whether the bird population is increasing or decreasing. This information helps Urbanek better manage yellow rails and their habitat at Seney National Wildlife Refuge. For instance, if yellow rails were decreasing in number, he might set aside additional areas where the birds could live and breed, undisturbed by people visiting the refuge.

Banding birds that evening in Michigan was just another night of work for field biologist Richard Urbanek. But for me it was a tremendous thrill. Over the years, I have been privileged to work closely with rare animals and with the remarkable scientists who study them. Often, I am amazed by the creative methods these scientists use to study animals. Answering simple questions such as Where does an animal go? What does it do all day? can quickly become complex when dealing with wild creatures. Finding out about a sloth that lives high in a tree, a squid that swims deep in the ocean, or a bird that travels thousands of miles can be challenging, indeed.

In this book, I focus on field scientists and researchers—those who study animals primarily in the wild, not in the laboratory. My aim is to sketch out some of the main challenges field scientists face. I also describe a few ways they overcome obstacles and obtain the information they need.

This book is dedicated to these field scientists, in the hope they find the courage, the creativity, the stamina, and the funding to continue their studies.

CAUTION: Only the activities mentioned in activity boxes are designed to be carried out by students. The other animal tracking, marking, and study techniques described in this book could be hazardous and should be used only by qualified scientists.

The federal government prohibits hunting, trapping, or harassing endangered and threatened species, marine mammals, bald eagles, golden eagles, hawks and owls, seabirds, songbirds, and other nongame migratory birds. Game birds such as ducks can be caught only during hunting season with a permit. Be sure to check with state and national officials before disturbing wild animals, because capturing, tagging, or otherwise handling such animals may be illegal without a permit.

1

HOOTING FOR OWLS AND SEARCHING FOR SQUID

How Scientists Find Wild Animals

In order for scientists to study wild animals, they have to find them first. That's often difficult. Even an animal as big as a blue whale is hard to find in an ocean. Small, quick-moving animals such as hummingbirds can dart away before you have a chance to get a good look at them. Many animals are also camouflaged, meaning they match their surroundings. You could stare hard and never see a greenish sloth in a leafy tree. And keen senses allow bears, wild cats, and other animals to hear you, smell you, and run away before you even know they're near.

So what do scientists do to find wild animals? Clever, occasionally wacky things. Take spotted owls, for instance. Perched high in trees, these speckled, bark-colored birds can be hard to find. In flight they are almost noiseless. One thing, however, can give away their location. If you hoot, they may hoot back. So that's what scientists do. They go out and hoot for owls, to locate the owls and their nests.

To find other animals, scientists vary their search techniques. They wade through swamps, climb trees, and scuba dive. They'll sit for days in the desert, just watching a waterhole, in case a bighorn sheep comes to drink. A few scientists even swim with sharks or wrestle giant snakes. Courageous, creative, perhaps a little kooky, field scientists will do almost anything to find the animals they seek.

TRACKING TECHNIQUES

Speckled and bark-colored, spotted owls blend with the scenery around them and can be difficult to locate by sight.

Do you know a raccoon by its smell? A deer by its tracks? The difference between the call of a tree frog and the call of a bird? To find animals, many field scientists work like detectives, looking for natural clues. A broken seashell, a track in the mud, even a clump of fur hanging on a thorn may lead them to the animal they seek. Sight, sound, smell, and even touch can help them find the animals they study.

WHAT A SIGHT Finding animals takes practice. In time, scientists develop what's called a "search image" of the animal they seek. For instance, a person studying hawks knows to look for the lumpy outline of a hawk sitting in a tree. That particular shape may catch their eye even if they're driving along a highway at high speed. Over the years, field scientists get better at finding their study animals. They begin to know a species not just by its obvious markings, but by its silhouette or by the way it moves.

ON THE RIGHT TRACK Tracking is often used to locate wild animals. To find and follow Amur leopards in Siberia, three biologists from the Hornocker Wildlife Research Institute in Idaho joined with their Russian colleagues to follow the cats' tracks through the snows of eastern Siberia. The purpose of the study was to find out how much wilderness the leopards needed to survive. So each day the biologists followed an individual cat's tracks, to see how far it traveled. (To track the animals, they also used radio collaring, which is discussed in Chapter 4.) Often, the biologists could tell which animal was which by the features of their tracks. For instance, the size of the tracks gave them an idea of the animals' body sizes. Blood in one track indicated one cat's foot was injured.

The leopards left other signs, too. They sometimes urinate and scratch the ground to mark their territories. (Territories are the areas, often around feeding or breeding spots, that individual animals will defend.) These scratch marks, which can differ among individuals, gave the biologists additional clues about which animal's tracks they were following. This study was only one of many that will be needed to find out how much land the leopards need.

PROFESSIONAL POOPER SCOOPERS   Every day, all over the world, scientists are looking for poop: scat, feces, droppings, or whatever you want to call it. Scat is an important part of many field studies. (There's even a word for the science of studying animal droppings: scatology.) To find an animal, scientists

---

ANIMAL-FINDING HINTS

In a crowded shopping mall or on a city street, we are bombarded by sights and sounds. To survive in these noisy, busy environments, people unconsciously ignore some of the sights and sounds around them. They have to so they can focus on what they're doing, whether that's driving down the road, walking to school, or listening to a conversation.

In the wild, however, people need finely tuned senses to detect animals. That's why experienced naturalists, birdwatchers, field scientists, and hunters tend to have eyes skilled in looking for motion. If they see something move out of the corner of their eye, they quickly check to see if it is an animal they seek. Others might unconsciously dismiss such motion. They might not notice a branch shaking and the monkey nearby that shook it.

Detecting animal sounds is also a skill that can be developed, because humans, to a degree, can focus on or ignore sounds as they do sights. For example, many people are so used to airplanes flying overhead that they no longer notice the noise. The same thing can happen at a noisy party, when you "tune in" to the voice of the person you are talking to, even when others are talking loudly nearby. Field scientists simply learn to concentrate on certain animal sounds, instead of other noises in their environment.

learn to identify the scat of the animal they are seeking. Then they look for that scat to locate paths the animals travel and the places where they spend time. Later, the scientists can stake out these spots, in hopes that the animals will return. Scientists also analyze scat, looking for hair, seeds, and other leftovers that tell them what the animals have eaten.

WHAT A SOUND   Last year, when I walked into an Ecuadorian rain forest, I was sure I heard trucks backing up. *Beep, beep, beep, beep* . . . the notes were exactly like the beeping noise trucks make when they're in reverse. Fortunately, our naturalist guide knew rain forest sounds better than I. He told me the beep was the call of a mannekin, a tiny bird. Soon he had located the bird, and we watched its comical, wing-flashing display. Our guide, like many ornithologists—scientists who study birds—knew bird species by their songs and calls.

To hone your animal-finding skills and find out more about your senses, try the following activities:

- Use a tape recorder to record outdoor noises in your neighborhood. Were you surprised by some sounds that sounded louder or softer than you expected? Did you hear any natural sounds, such as insects buzzing, chipmunks clucking, or birds calling in the background? Try to listen more closely to them.

- Outdoors, preferably in a natural area, spend a minute looking straight ahead. But concentrate on the scenes to the sides of your main field of view. This "side vision" is called your peripheral vision. Often, you may sense motion with your peripheral vision. If you see motion, turn and look more closely in that area. This will help you to detect animals even if they aren't right in front of you.

- Learn how to use "search images" for animals. Choose a type of animal that is common in your area. (A squirrel, a pigeon, or a robin will do.) Think about the animal's shape and size. Keep that image locked in your mind. Then quickly scan trees, fields, and lawns for that animal. Try to ignore the rest of the scene. Practice doing this activity daily and in new areas. Switch to search images of less common animals. You may be surprised at how your animal-finding skills improve!

These scientists can walk into a forest and immediately know most of the bird species that are present and sometimes what they are doing, just by their sounds.

Sounds are also useful for identifying other animals, such as frogs. My husband and I once helped survey frog species in the Great Lakes region. First, by listening to a tape recording, we memorized the calls of frog species in our area. Then, we went out and listened to frogs calling in marshes, and we made a list of which species we heard.

Insects, too, can sometimes be identified by their sounds. Dr. Vincent G. Dethier, in his book *Crickets, Katydids, Concerts, and Solos,* describes his adventures seeking crickets in New England forests and fields. He learned to distinguish among the sounds made by cricket species common to the area. Once, in order to track down a cricket making a particularly unusual noise, he even ventured into a graveyard late at night. The local sheriff and deputy grabbed him, thinking he was vandalizing graves! Fortunately, he managed to convince them he really was studying crickets, and they did not take him to jail.

Owl Pellet Clues

Owl pellets look a little like dog scat, but they aren't. Pellets come from an owl's other end. Owls swallow their prey whole. Their bodies digest the meaty parts. Then they cough up a pellet containing fur and bone. Piles of pellets are often found underneath an owl's favorite roost.

To find out what owls eat, scientists tease apart these pellets using small metal probes or picks. Then, bone-by-bone, they figure out what animals the owls have eaten. Biological supply companies sell owl pellets that are sterilized and tool kits to pull the pellets apart. Students can order kits and try owl pellet dissection for themselves. For owl pellet kits, contact:

Genesis Inc.
P.O. Box 2242
Mt. Vernon, WA 98273
1-800-4-PELLET
1-800-473-5538

Scientists find some lemurs by looking for them at night with headlamps. The animals' eyes glow, reflecting the light of the searchers' lamps.

Late one night in a rain forest in Madagascar, an island off the coast of Africa, two glowing eyes peered down at me. If I hadn't been looking for them, I might have been scared. But the scientists I was with reassured me that the eyes belonged to an avahi, a type of lemur we sought. (Lemurs are an ancient kind of primate. Some lemurs are nocturnal, meaning they are active at night.) For hours, we'd been searching for animals by walking through the forest, shining flashlights and headlamps—lights we wore on our heads—up into the trees. We were hoping our lights would flash on an animal's eyes, which may shine even when the rest of its body blends in with the darkness.

A lemur's eyes or a house cat's eyes glow at night in the glare of a flashlight's beam. Light enters their pupils and reflects back, bouncing the light back toward the observer. Certain other animals, such as alligators, spiders, and primates, have eyes that reflect light, too. Scientists, like the ones I was with, use this to their advantage. They search at night, scanning trees, underbrush, or water, with their flashlights and headlamps. In this way, they can find many nocturnal animals that stay well hidden during the day. Researchers can sometimes identify the kind of animal by the size of the eyes and how far apart they are. Looking for shining eyes is just one of the "bright ideas" scientists use to find animals.

GREAT GLOWING SCORPIONS!   Scorpions are often the color of the sand or rocks where they live. They hide in crannies and crevices during the day. So looking for these arachnids would be tough if scientists hadn't figured out the scorpions' "secret": scorpions glow in the dark! Well, actually, they only glow in the dark if you shine a special light, called a black light, on them. The black light gives off ultraviolet light—light with high-frequency wavelengths. (It's the same type of light that makes fluorescent rocks glow purple and green in museum displays.) The light rays cannot be seen by people, so even if the light is shining, it seems dark. The ultraviolet light makes the scorpions' bodies glow.

To find scorpions, Dr. Gary Polis, a professor at Vanderbilt University, walks in the desert at night and shines a black light on the ground. Then Polis and his colleagues carefully pick up the glowing scorpions using foot-long tweezers, to avoid the scorpions' pincers and stingers. Those stingers, how-

Two scorpions fighting under ultraviolet light seem to glow in the dark.

A Master Bird-Finder

Imagine being able to identify more than three thousand bird species just by their calls. One famous field biologist, Ted Parker, could do just that. He's been called "the greatest field biologist of the 20th century." Parker was the director of the Rapid Assessment Program (RAP) sponsored by Conservation International, a nonprofit environmental group. In the early 1990s, Parker and other RAP team biologists flew to remote tropical areas that were threatened with destruction. In a matter of weeks, these experts would survey each forest and find out, in general, what kinds of birds, frogs, insects, and plants lived there.

Parker listened to and recorded the bird sounds he heard in the forest. Later, he could play back the tapes and identify any bird sounds he had missed. Sometimes he could also compare the recordings with others he had made, to figure out difficult identifications. In general, identifying birds by sound is much faster than trying to find and identify them by sight. That's especially true in rain forests, where birds are often high in trees or hidden by leaves, so they're hard to see and to identify.

Using the information from the RAP scientists, Conservation International helped conserve rain forest areas. They gathered support from government and conservation groups to protect the areas that had the greatest biodiversity—the greatest number of different species.

Unfortunately, during an expedition to Ecuador in August 1993, Ted Parker was killed in a plane crash, along with several other RAP team members. Scientists mourn the loss of all these highly skilled researchers. But other scientists have taken up the work, and the RAP program continues today. It's just one of the many programs in which field scientists use sight, sound, and other senses to look for and identify animals and plants.

ever, aren't the only danger for Polis and his assistants. A major problem is poisonous snakes. Snakes are also active at night in the desert. So the researchers must wear heavy boots and thick shields to guard their legs against snake bites.

SEARCHING FOR GIANT SQUID   In November 1996, Dr. Clyde Roper, a zoologist at the Smithsonian's National Museum of Natural History, embarked on a voyage to study giant squid. The only problem was no one had ever seen a giant squid alive in the wild! Giant squid, which can be up to 60 feet (18.3 meters) long, live in deep oceans. But they are known mostly from dead carcasses washed up on beaches and caught in fishing nets. Tidbits of giant squid have also been found in the stomachs of sperm whales.

Whales may be the key to Dr. Roper's study, because they apparently eat lots of giant squid. Dr. Roper is hoping the whales will lead him to the squid. Near New Zealand, he's been tagging along after sperm whales and listening in on their sounds to find out when they're feeding. Once at a feeding spot, Roper climbs into a submersible, an underwater vehicle, and dives deep into the ocean and searches. So far he hasn't fulfilled his lifelong dream, by finding a giant squid. But his study and his search continues.

BAITS AND TRICKS

Sometimes the easiest way to find wild animals is to have them find you. Many scientists use bait. Bait can be a food, a scent, a light—anything that will bring an animal closer.

FRUITY ATTRACTIONS AND NIGHT LIGHTS   To attract insects, scientists use many different lures. Setting out mashed, decaying fruit is an easy way to attract fruit flies and wasps. Meat scraps are almost sure to bring in flies and beetles.

Light traps are perfect for capturing light-seeking insects. Those are the kind that gather around streetlamps and porch lights at night. To catch them, an entomologist—a scientist who studies insects—rigs up a light, then stretches a white cloth, such as a sheet, a couple of feet in front of it. The insects fly toward the light and land on the illuminated sheet. There, they can easily be picked off the fabric and studied. Using a black light, instead of a regular light, can be good for attracting certain moths. And if they don't have other equipment handy, entomologists have been known to just park their cars and turn on the headlights to see what the light attracts!

A "DIRTY" TRICK Finding insects that are ground dwellers requires a different technique. Scientists construct a Berlese funnel—a simple device. A funnel is set in the top of a jar, and a light is hung over the funnel. The funnel is filled with leaf litter and soil. The light heats and dries the material at the top of the funnel. Any insects in the material crawl away from the heat, light, or dryness. This leads them downward. Eventually, they fall out of the funnel into the jar, where scientists can study them.

DON'T CALL US, WE'LL CALL YOU To lure wild animals, field biologists may play recordings of animal calls. Using this technique, my husband and I recently surveyed marsh birds for a study of birds near the Great Lakes. We walked into marshes and played a tape recording of a grebe's—a type of water bird's—call. In each marsh, after playing the call, we waited five minutes. If the grebes were nearby, they would call in response. If the birds called, we would write down how many we heard calling.

Birds sing to attract mates and also to mark their territory. So in response to taped calls, birds may call, sing, fly out into the open, and make feather-fluffing, wing-flapping, displays. That's great for scientists, who get a good look at the birds. But it's not so great for the birds, who end up spending time singing and displaying to attract a mate or fend off a rival that's not really there. That's why scientists minimize their use of recordings. They are concerned that birds that are disturbed might neglect other activities, such as taking care of chicks or eggs.

WHAT'S THAT SMELL? Have you ever seen a dog urinate on a fire hydrant or bush? It was probably just marking its territory. This mark is like a "smell signpost" that tells other animals whose territory it is or what animals have visited there. Monkeys, dogs, and cats mark their territories with scents. Researchers and photographers sometimes take advantage of this habit. For example, in central Africa, a photographer poured leopard urine onto a forest trail. (Before traveling to Africa, he had collected the urine from a leopard in a zoo.) He set up a camera that would be triggered if a leopard walked through a laser beam. One night, sure enough, a leopard came to investigate the "stranger's"—the zoo leopard's—smell. The camera snapped its photo. Other scents, such as smelly foods, are also used to lure animals. Dead catfish have been used to attract eels. Strawberry jam has been used to lure brown bears!

PEOPLE BAIT Most people wouldn't want to look for giant leeches, which are 8-inch (20-centimeter) long, blood-sucking creatures. But researchers from the University of California mounted an expedition to do just that. Leeches can be useful for laboratory studies and even for some medical procedures, so the scientists needed a supply of them. To find leeches, the scientists traveled all the way to French Guiana and used nets to sweep through slow-moving waters. But it was no use; they could not find a single leech. Finally, a local boy showed them the best leech-catching technique. He waded into the water, stood there for a while, and the leeches attached themselves to his skin! With a few tugs and a squirt of lemon juice, he was able to remove the leeches. (Leeches, if left on for very long, will bite a person and feed on their blood.) Once the scientists adopted the boy's technique, they had as many leeches as they needed. Using the leeches they gathered, they can now breed leeches in captivity instead of capturing them from the wild.

A MATTER OF HABIT

Using tricks, traps, and keen senses, field scientists can usually find the animals they seek, even at a new study site. But these searches take time. An easier way to find an animal is to know its behavior and its habitat well. Animals, like humans, tend to have daily routines. A hummingbird may have a flower route and visit certain bushes and trees and flowers, in sequence, every hour. Red squirrels have favorite eating spots. Underneath these perches you'll find piles of gnawed walnut shells. Ants create trails, even spending time maintaining these tiny highways by clearing away debris. Once scientists know animals' habits, they can stake out the areas the animals frequent in order to observe them.

2

THE ART OF
COUNTING CARIBOU

How Scientists Identify, Count, and Measure Wild Animals

What kind of insects live on Miami beaches? How many lions are there in Africa? How long can a python grow? To answer these and other questions, field scientists must identify, measure, and count wild animals. These activities may sound simple; but they're not. Just try identifying a beetle, weighing an elephant, or counting all the ants in your backyard. You'll quickly discover what a challenge field studies can be!

WHAT *IS* THAT?: THE PROBLEM OF IDENTIFICATION

Sometimes the problem isn't finding a wild animal. It's figuring out what animal you've found! Young bald eagles, for instance, don't have the white heads and white tails of adult bald eagles. Finch species in the Galápagos Islands may differ only slightly, most often in the size of their beaks. Some birds, such as flycatchers, look so much alike, they're best told apart by their calls. In many cases, scientists use a variety of clues to piece together an animal's identity.

A KEY POINT   To identify an organism, some scientists use a taxonomic key. The word *taxonomic* comes from *taxonomy*, the science of naming things. A taxonomic key is a list of questions scientists ask themselves about an organism they have found. Answering each question narrows the possibilities for the organism's identity. Step-by-step, the questions lead the scientist to the organism's proper name and classification, or category. By using a key, a scientist can most accurately identify an animal. But it takes a lot of time. Once scientists are familiar with the basics of a key, they may skip some of the question steps.

FIELD MARKS AND FIELD GUIDES   Another tool for identifying animals is a field guide. Field guides are books that contain drawings, photos, and descriptions of animals. They present much of the same information that is in a taxonomic key, but in a different form. Unlike taxonomic keys, field guides focus on features that can be seen from observation in the wild. (Taxonomic keys may rely on characteristics that are only obvious close-up, when animals are observed or measured under laboratory conditions.) Field guides list field marks, characteristics that can be seen in the field and that distinguish one animal from similar species, or kinds, of animals. For a bird, that may be the color of the head, the shape of the tail, or other features.

Field guides are essential tools for identifying animals such as the bird seen in this photograph.

THE NAME GAME   Woodchuck and whistle pig are two of the many names for the furry mammal that pokes its nose out of its hole on Groundhog Day. Like many other animals, groundhogs have several different common names. Common names can vary from region to region and language to language. That causes problems for scientists. For example, the bird that Americans call a "robin" is not the same bird species the British call a "robin." And in the western United States, someone who mentions a "groundhog" may be talking about a prairie dog, instead!

    To avoid such confusion, scientists give organisms scientific names. These names are used by scientists worldwide, no matter what language they speak. By using scientific names, scientists can be sure that they're talking about the same animal or plant or fungus.

Scientific names reflect scientific classifications—the categories into which scientists group organisms, based on their similarities. The largest category is a kingdom. Kingdoms include the plant kingdom and the animal kingdom. Within a kingdom there are subgroupings: phylum, class, order, family, genus, species, and subspecies. An animal's scientific name is made up of its genus name plus its species name. For instance, a red-tailed hawk is called *Buteo jamaicensis* because *buteo* is the genus and *jamaicensis* is the species. (These names are always italicized or underlined, and the genus name is always capitalized.) Some animals also have a third name added, to indicate their subspecies. For example, *Buteo jamaicensis harlani* is the Harlan's subspecies of the red-tailed hawk.

A researcher examines a beetle with a magnifying lens in order to identify it. Could it be a new species?

AHA! IT'S NEW! Every year, field scientists find animals they think may be "new" species—species never before identified, scientifically. (That doesn't mean, of course, that no one has ever seen or named the animals. Often, native people have known about these animals for years.) In 1990 scientists found a new species of primate, called the black-faced lion tamarin, on an island near São Paulo, Brazil. And in 1996 a new kind of sunbird was found in the Phillippines. When scientists find an animal they believe is new to science, they must go through a long process before the animal is officially recognized and named. They take notes about where and when the animal was found and what color it is. They also photograph, tape record, and video-tape the animal and its calls if possible. In most, but not all cases, a few individuals of the species are collected, killed, and preserved. These are called specimens.

The specimens will be studied carefully by scientists in labs. They take many measurements of the animal's body, such as the length of its legs, arms, wings, feathers, fins, or toes. They compare the specimens with similar specimens from museums and universities worldwide. Months or even years may pass before field scientists can prove they have discovered a new species. When they do, they can give it a name, which must be approved by other scientists in their specialty.

DNA DEVELOPMENTS In recent years, scientists have added another step to their taxonomic studies. They now take skin samples from the animals. From these samples, scientists extract deoxyribonucleic acid (DNA), which is genetic material. By comparing one animal's DNA to another animal's DNA, scientists can tell how closely the animals are related. When animals are very rare, DNA studies may be used instead of capturing and killing the animals for specimens.

MEASURE BY MEASURE

Once scientists have identified an animal, their next job is usually to measure it. But how do you measure a python? (Very carefully . . .) How do you weigh a hummingbird? These are the kinds of questions that must be answered by field scientists in their work.

METRIC MEASURES In the United States, most people use the English system of measurement. They measure length in inches and yards, mass in pounds, and area in acres. Worldwide, most other countries use the metric system of measurement. In metric, you measure length in centimeters and meters, mass in kilograms, and area in hectares. Metric measurements are the standard used by scientists all over the world. Scientists in the United States use the metric system, too. Using scientific names and metric measurements allows scientists to communicate clearly about their work.

TOOLS OF THE TRADE   To measure animals, field scientists use many different tools. In field camps, scientists may use a balance scale, like the ones used in laboratories. But even more often, they use a spring scale, which is lighter and easier to carry. You may have seen a spring scale hanging in a supermarket's vegetable aisle. To use it, you place whatever you want to weigh in the hanging pan. The material pulls down on a hidden spring. And up above, the weight registers on a scale.

To use a spring scale out in the field, scientists place a study animal in a container or a sling. Then they hang the container or sling from the spring scale. (Beforehand, mountain lions, bears, and other large animals are anesthetized—injected with drugs that make them sleepy—for easier handling.) Spring scales and slings have been used to measure everything from tiny mice to large dolphins.

Measuring the length of an
anaconda is easier said than done!

TOO TWISTY   Giant anacondas, snakes that can be 12 feet (3.7 meters) or more long, present a real measurement challenge. These muscular snakes tend to twist into coils. They won't stretch out, allowing scientists to measure their

24

length. To solve this dilemma, two researchers hold the anaconda. An assistant runs a string along the snake's backbone, tracing its twists and curves. Once done, they can straighten the string and measure it. . . . And voila! They've measured the snake's body length.

HUMDINGER OF A PROBLEM Hummingbirds can weigh less than a penny. They fly quickly and are hard to catch. So researchers know from the start that weighing hummingbirds will be a difficult enterprise. To make things even harder, scientists may need to weigh a single hummingbird repeatedly throughout the day. That way they can see how the bird's weight changes as it feeds and flies. In one study, researchers came up with a particularly clever method for weighing hummingbirds. They noticed one bird had a favorite perch. So they rigged a scale under the perch. After that, each time the bird landed on the perch, its weight was measured and recorded!

This tiny hummingbird weighs in at just 3 grams, and its nest is smaller than a golf ball.

Field scientists often have to improvise. Here two researchers use a knit cap to hold a bear cub they are weighing.

Weighing something as large as this polar bear calls for special equipment—a helicopter!

LEARNING TO COUNT

Counting hundreds of thousands of caribou (a type of deer) on Alaska's tundra is not a simple proposition. To do it, wildlife biologists fly in planes back and forth over the tundra, for several weeks. They take several hundred photographs to document the vast herds of caribou. Then back in the lab, they literally have to count the dots—the tiny caribou pictured in the aerial photographs. One caribou, two caribou . . . counting takes months of hard work, before they have a total. Biologists like to keep an eye on the number of caribou, to make sure the population remains large and healthy. But counting caribou is easy compared with counting some other animals . . .

COMMON "CENSUS" To census, or count animals, scientists often mark off a grid, like the squares on graph paper. A grid makes counting more manageable. It's much easier to count the animals in each square and add those numbers than to count the animals all at once. Sometimes scientists make a real grid by marking a field with strings strung between stakes. Or they may use an imaginary grid, or mark a grid on an aerial photograph. Aerial surveys are used to count not only caribou, but also elephants, bison, and musk oxen.

GET YOUR DUCKS IN A ROW
In many cases, counting all the animals in a population is just not possible. Biologists have neither the time nor the money to count every duck in Canada and the United States. Yet

How many caribou do you see in this picture?

knowing the number of ducks is important. Counting ducks helps government biologists gauge the health of the duck population. Each year they consider these numbers when deciding how many ducks of each species can be shot by hunters that season.

As a result, each year biologists from the U.S. Fish and Wildlife Service and the Canadian Wildlife Service carry out a limited count of ducks. They fly planes over paths called transects—long, straight routes. Flying low, they count the birds of each species as fast as they can. Many ducks are missed. But the numbers are still useful, because Canadian and American biologists have

IN SEARCH OF HIDDEN ELEPHANTS

How do you count elephants in a deep, dark rain forest? It sounds like an elephant joke, but it's not. It's a serious question that Richard and Karen Barnes, two researchers working for Wildlife Conservation International, faced in their work. They studied elephants in the rain forests of Gabon, a country in western Africa. In Gabon's forests, it's hard to see elephants because of the trees and thick undergrowth. Because of the trees, low-flying planes cannot census the forest elephants as they do on the savannas, where there are fewer trees.

The Barneses' study began in 1985. They often heard the elephants, yet they rarely saw them. But it was important that they count them, somehow, because conservationists needed to find out how big the population was. They were concerned that too many elephants were being killed for their ivory tusks and that the species was being threatened.

Eventually, the Barneses figured out a way to estimate the number of elephants. Instead of counting actual elephants, they counted elephant scat. From other scientists' work, they knew that an elephant defecates—produces droppings, about seventeen times per day. They divided the number of fresh elephant droppings they found by seventeen, to determine the number of elephants in the area. Their two-year study, plus the work of other researchers, showed that the population of forest elephants was quite large. As late as 1990, they estimated sixty-nine thousand elephants lived in the country of Gabon.

been counting ducks on these routes since 1955. They can't say they have counted every duck. But by doing the count, in the same way, every year, they come up with numbers that can show trends. Some years the numbers are higher or lower than before. These numbers give them an idea of how duck populations are doing.

ANIMAL "CALLING CARDS"   Scientists don't always count animals by sight. They may use other clues. Tracks, nests, calls, and other signs are also used by scientists to estimate the number of animals. For instance, researchers sometimes count wolf and coyote howls to estimate the size of those populations. And biologists take a census of endangered Kirtland's warblers by walking along marked plots and counting the number of males they hear singing songs.

Measuring birds' beaks, and monitoring changes in beak size, can yield important information about evolution.

WHY MEASUREMENTS MATTER

Scientists use measurements for a wide range of applications. Peter Grant and Rosemary Grant, a husband-and-wife research team, measure birds' beaks to study evolution. When they're not busy teaching at Princeton University, the Grants are measuring finches on a small island in the Pacific Ocean. Every year since 1972, they and their assistants have measured the beaks of finches on Daphne Major, an island near Ecuador. Their study has looked at how the finch population's average beak size has changed from year to year. Their research on birds' beaks has shown that evolution can occur much more rapidly than scientists previously thought.

Other measurements made by scientists have conservation uses. The number of snakes, snails, lizards, or other animals must be determined before scientists are sure a particular animal species is rare enough to need protection. The weight and length of a mountain lion, a fish, or a monkey can also be an indication of its health. (If an animal is not eating enough or is diseased, its body measurements may decrease.) Changes in animals' measurements give conservationists an early warning that an animal species may be in danger. For these and other reasons, it is important that field scientists make the most accurate measurements they can.

3

KNOWING A ZEBRA
BY ITS STRIPES

How Scientists Mark and Recognize Individual Animals

To learn about animals' lives, scientists often study the same group of animals over many years. This helps them find out about animals' behaviors, especially how they act in family groups. Long-term studies investigate questions such as which animals mate with one another, what foods they choose, and how they raise their young. Long-term studies may also examine how animals inherit characteristics such as color, beak length, or fin shape.

For these studies, it's not enough for scientists to watch elephants, or fruit flies, in general. Scientists need to be able to identify individual animals: fruit fly A, or fruit fly B, or the elephant with the short tusks. Each time scientists see an animal, they need to know if it is one they have seen before. So scientists keep records, like family histories. They record births or deaths. They keep track of which animals are related to one another, and how animal families grow and change, year by year.

USING NATURAL MARKERS

Like a person's fingerprint, a zebra's stripe pattern is unique. No two zebras have the same pattern. Some have more stripes, some have fewer stripes, some have thicker, thinner, or incomplete stripes. By photographing zebras and laying the photos side by side, scientists can tell which zebra is which. Below are some clues scientists use to tell other animals apart.

TALES TAILS TELL   When you observe a humpback whale from a whale-watching boat, you often see only its back, its flippers, or its tail. The rest of the whale is hidden underwater. Nevertheless, biologists can tell whales apart by their appearance. Dark and light patches, notches, and scars on the whales' tails help scientists distinguish one whale tail from another. By photographing whales' tails, biologists have cataloged many of the whales that visit Stellwagen Banks, a rich feeding ground off the New England coast. Now they can recognize the whales that visit year after year.

LISTEN TO THAT ACCENT   After studying a killer whale named Corky at Marineland in Los Angeles, Alexandra Morton decided to track down and study Corky's family in the wild. She was curious about how killer whales communicated with one another through clicks and other calls. She hoped her research on Corky's calls in captivity would help her understand Corky's family's calls in the wild. The problem was that the people who captured Corky had only vague ideas about where his pod—his family and other whales he traveled with—lived.

Fortunately, scientist Michael Bigg of Canada's Pacific Biological Station had been studying killer whales, also called orcas, for years. He and his assis-

No two zebras have the same stripes! That means scientists can tell them apart.

Photographs of whale tails, which each have individual markings, can help researchers to identify a particular whale.

tants had photographed the dorsal fins—the fins on the top of the backs—of many of the orcas that lived along the coast of Washington State and British Columbia. It was in this region that Corky had been captured. By studying a photo of Corky, Bigg was able to pinpoint a pod of whales that had similar markings on their dorsal fins. Then Alexandra Morton could locate the wild whales. Once she had listened to their underwater calls, she was sure these were members of Corky's family. Not only do orcas have distinctive markings, they have distinctive dialects, too. Whales that live in different regions of the ocean sound slightly different and use slightly different calls and whistles. More and more, scientists are discovering that individual animals have distinctive voices. Sandhill cranes and bald eagles now can be recognized individually by the sound of their calls.

CHECK OUT THOSE NOSES AND EARS!   If you know noses, you can tell gorillas apart. At least that's what Dian Fossey decided. She was the world-famous primatologist whose life story was told in the movie *Gorillas in the Mist*. For eighteen years, Fossey studied mountain gorillas on the steep, forest-covered slopes of the Virunga volcanoes in Rwanda. She learned to distinguish individual gorillas from one another by the ridges on their noses.

In the case of elephants, noses don't help much. But long ago, Dr. Cynthia Moss discovered that ears did. Moss, the director of the Amboseli Elephant Research Project, has been studying elephants in Africa for more than twenty-five years. She sketches elephants' ears and takes photographs of them from several different angles. By looking at the ear shape, plus any rips, warts, and notches in the ears, she is able to tell individual elephants apart.

Joyce Poole, who worked with Moss, describes the process of getting to know the elephants in her book *Coming of Age With Elephants:*

> There were small ears, big ears, smooth ears, ragged ears, round ears, flop ears, curtain ears, and crumpled ears; there were ears with any combination of flap cuts, scoop cuts, V cuts, wedges, nicks, notches, tears . . . Tusks, too were different . . . With time I began to see that, just like people, each elephant also had a different body shape and face, and that there were strong family resemblances between sisters and between mothers and daughters.

What's in a Name?

It depends on who you ask. To keep track of individual animals, scientists must identify them with a name, number, or letter code. For a long time, the scientific community frowned on giving study animals personal names, such as Larry or Liz. They felt that naming the animals would lead researchers to look on the animals more as pets instead of study subjects. This, they believed, would interfere with scientific study, because researchers might begin giving animals credit for emotions and thoughts researchers could not prove they had.

Nevertheless, Jane Goodall, the famous primatologist who studied chimpanzees for more than thirty years in Tanzania, named the animals in her study. The names of the chimps—Flo, Fifi, Flint, and others—became known in the pages of *National Geographic* and other magazines that featured her work. Still, like the names used by other scientists for their study subjects, Goodall's chimps' names were initially rejected by the scientific community. In the 1960s, one scientific journal asked her to alter an article she had written by changing the names of the chimps to numbers. She refused to make the changes, but they published the article, after all.

Most biologists, in scientific journals, still refer to the animals in their studies by number and letter codes. However, among scientists in research camps, study animals inevitably acquire nicknames.

NAMES AND CODES Dr. Moss uses a combination of names and codes to identify the hundreds of elephants she has studied. Each family has a two-letter code such as AB or HH. In addition, the elephants have names starting with the first letter of the family code. For example, elephants in family GB have names such as Gloria, Gladys, and Golda. For computer records and field notes, adult females also have a shorter, three-letter code, based on their name. Baby elephants are identified by their mother's three-letter code and the year of their birth. Only if they survive their first few, dangerous years are they given a name and letter code of their own. This complex system has helped elephant researchers track the elephants over several decades.

TAKE A CLOSER LOOK   Whether you're looking at gigantic giraffes or minuscule moths, it takes patience and close observation to figure out the differences between individuals. Almost every year, scientists come up with new techniques to do the job. Just recently, they discovered that the pineal eye, a spot on the top of a sea turtle's head, has a pattern that's unique to each individual turtle. It may soon be used to tell sea turtles apart. Now if scientists could only figure out what the pineal eye does!

USING ARTIFICIAL MARKERS

Most animals probably have natural features to tell one another apart. But these differences aren't always easily distinguished by human observers, especially from a distance. Consequently, some scientists mark animals artificially. Brands, tags, radio collars, notches, and recently, microchips, have been used to mark individual animals so scientists can recognize and track them.

BIRDS WITH BRACELETS   Probably the best-known animal marking is the bird band. Bird bands are tiny metal or plastic identification bracelets that researchers put on birds' legs. These bands have numbers and sometimes combinations of colors, as well.

Bird bands come in different sizes, meant to fit small-, medium-, and large-sized birds!

Each year, during migration, amateur birdwatchers around the United States help scientists capture and band wild birds. These bird banders are specially trained and certified to do the job. (It is illegal to capture native, wild birds without a permit.) Bird banders capture birds by setting up mist nets—thin, almost invisible mesh nets. The birds fly into the nets and become entangled. Periodically, the banders check the nets and remove the birds. The birds are usually unharmed except for a few lost feathers. The banders may band the birds right away or slip them into small cloth bags to take them to another spot for weighing, measuring, and banding.

In the United States, the Fish and Wildlife Service keeps a national database of banding records. The banders turn in records of where birds are banded and where they are recaptured or observed. Colors and numbers on the bands help scientists identify individual birds and how far they have traveled.

THIS TAG IS NOT A GAME Birds are not the only animals marked by scientists. Other animals are marked, many with specially designed tags. To tag

IF YOU FIND AN ANIMAL WITH A TAG OR BAND

If you find a bird with a band, or another animal with a special marking, take note. If you can get close to the animal safely, or see the markings through binoculars, write down any information on the band. Taking note of bands on dead animals is important, too. Write down where you found the animal, what condition it was in, and the date and time you found it. The band may list a place to contact, but if not, call the U.S. Fish and Wildlife Service, state fish and game department, your local nature center, Audubon Club, or the biology department at a local university. They may be able to tell you where to send the information you have gathered.

Information from bird bands and other markings can be very important to scientists. If you take the time and trouble to write down this information and send it in, you can help in scientific studies. Information from banded birds found all over the world has helped scientists learn where birds migrate and how far and how fast they travel.

If you look closely you can see that this butterfly has been tagged #67752, and the tag was put on in Los Angeles, California.

monk seals, researchers use a hole punch—the kind used to make holes in leather belts. They make a small hole in the webbing between the bones of the seal's flippers. A plastic plug, like a large earring stud, is put through the hole and fastened. Attached to the plug is a plastic, numbered tag.

Believe it or not, tags are also used to identify and track butterflies. Tiny, numbered paper tags are glued to the wings of monarch butterflies, to track these insects' migrations. Each year, tens of thousands of monarchs are tagged by volunteers who work in a nationwide tagging program called Monarch Watch. The information from these tags is helping to solve mysteries about where and when monarchs travel. (For information on how you can participate in Monarch Watch, read the "You Can Get Involved" section near the end of this book.)

1,2,3,4,5,6,7   On the TV show *Sesame Street* a man with a paint can walks around painting numbers on things. Scientist do, too. Only they paint numbers on snails, iguanas, and other animals! On the island of North Seymour, in the Galápagos Islands, you might see iguana number 12. A scientist painted numbers on many of the iguanas' backs in order to study their individual eating habits.

While walking through a forest in Madagascar, I spotted giant snails almost as big as tennis balls. Even stranger, some of the snails' shells had white numbers on them. I later discovered a scientist at a nearby research station had painted numbers on the snails so she could find out how far and how fast the snails travel. With a ribbon, she would mark the place where snail number 1 started. Then, hours later, she would check to see how far the snail had traveled.

Painting on numbers works fine for snails. But it isn't always practical. For starters, paint wears off. And you can't use paint on animals, such as frogs, that breathe through their skin. Poisonous chemicals in paint could be absorbed through the frog's skin and harm it. (For a similar reason, scientists make sure their hands are clean when handling frogs. Even a tiny bit of mosquito repellent could kill the frog if it got onto the frog's skin.)

DESIGNATED DOLPHINS   Scientists used to attach tags to dolphins' dorsal fins in order to mark them. But these tags did not stay on long. So today, instead, scientists take photographs to record the shape of dolphins' fins and any other distinguishing marks and scars. In addition, some researchers capture and freeze-brand dolphins. A supercooled metal brand in the shape of a numeral is briefly pressed against a dolphin's skin. This leaves a white mark. The numbering is useful because if the dolphins are accidentally caught in fishermen's nets or found dead on beaches, people may report the numbers to the scientists. Then the scientists can include the information on the fate of these dolphins in their studies.

SCALES, NOTCHES, AND CODES   How do you mark a snake? It's always been a puzzle. Paint wears off, tags tear off, and a collar could fall off or get in the snake's way. That's why researchers María Muñoz and Jesús Rivas mark giant anacondas by snipping off a few of the snakes' scales. These two Venezualan biologists are studying anacondas as part of their research to get their Ph.D.s (their doctoral degrees). One way they find their study subjects is by trudging through muddy swamps until they feel an anaconda underfoot!

Marking the snakes by snipping their scales doesn't harm them. Scales are made

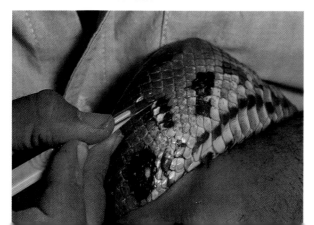

A scientist removes scales from an anaconda, so that this particular snake can be identified later.

of keratin, the same material human hair and fingernails are made of. The scales are removed in a specific pattern that identifies the snake by number. Near its tail, anaconda number 763 would have 7 scales snipped off on one side, 6 scales removed from another spot, and 3 removed from still another.

A number pattern is also used to mark Galápagos tortoises. Notches are filed into the lower edges of the tortoises' top shells. Notches in certain parts of the shell indicate numbers in the single digits; others indicate tens, hundreds, or thousands. For instance, tortoise number 2,741 would have a series of notches like these:

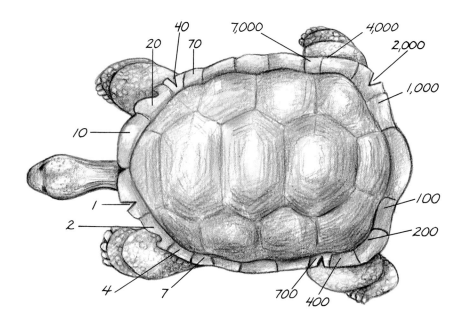

"HIVE"-TECH SOLUTIONS   Researchers used to glue numbered plastic dots on bees' backs. Why? So they could tell the bees apart. But even then, studying bees was difficult. It was hard to read the bees' numbers because they moved so quickly. Then Stephen Buschmann, an entomologist at the Carl Hayden Bee Research Center in Arizona, came up with a clever marking technique. At the entrance to a beehive, he rigged a scanner, similar to the ones used in super-

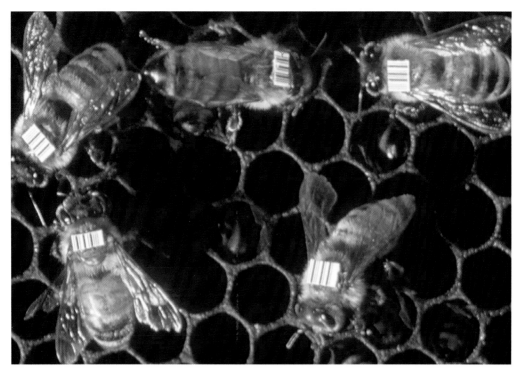

Scientists can keep track of an individual bee's movements with the help of a bar-coded tag on the bee and a scanner at the entrance to the beehive.

markets to check out groceries. He attached tiny bar codes, like the ones on grocery boxes, to the bees' backs. With these in place, the computer could scan the bees' tags and automatically record each bee's comings and goings! This helped Buschmann study and analyze the bees' behavior.

CAPTURING AND MARKING ANIMALS: A RISKY BUSINESS?

Capturing a bear, a bird, a dolphin, or just about any other wild animal, stresses that animal. The animal's heart may beat faster. The animal may struggle to escape. Birds batter their wings against cages. Vipers may strike, using valuable energy and poison to defend themselves. Scientists work to reduce this stress as much as possible when working to capture animals in the wild.

DRUGS AND DARTS   To reduce the rate of injury—to animals and to scientists—many researchers give large animals tranquilizers before attempting to work with them. Tranquilizers are drugs that calm the animal and make it fall asleep. For large mammals such as bears, monkeys, and deer, biologists use a gun to shoot a needle-tipped dart into the animal's hide. The dart is filled with a tranquilizer that is automatically injected. After darting, the scientists follow the animal until the tranquilizer takes effect. The animal must become sluggish enough for capture. Once it's captured, scientists work quickly to tag the animal. They may also measure it, weigh it, and take blood samples.

PREDATOR PATROL   Afterward, biologists usually retreat to a safe distance and watch the animal until it is fully active again. Why? Because a groggy, tranquilized animal is easy prey for predators. Scientists may even need to stand guard, as Mark and Delia Owens found out.

The Owenses, a husband-and-wife research team, left their studies at University of Georgia to study lions, hyenas, and jackals in Africa. (They even sold their stereo, television, and pots and pans to earn the money so they could go!) One night in the Kalahari desert, Mark and Delia tranquilized a jackal. It was recovering at their campsite, when Mark looked away from the jackal for a few short moments. When he looked back, seven lions had surrounded the jackal! He ended up having to drive off the lions by scaring them with his truck. (For the rest of the Owenses' exciting story, including how the lions ended up in Delia's tent, read their book *Cry of the Kalahari*.)

ARE TRANQUILIZERS TOO DANGEROUS?   Tranquilizers have been a great help in animal studies. But these drugs have their risks. A drug dosage that is slightly too much for an animal can kill it. If too little tranquilizer is used, the animal may injure itself or the biologists working with it. Estimating the right amount of tranquilizer, according to the individual animal's body size, can be difficult. When using the drugs on animal species never before tranquilized, the risks are even greater.

For this reason, scientists do not always choose to capture and mark animals. Biruté Galdikas, a famous primatologist, began studying wild orangutans in the swampy jungles of Borneo in 1971 and continues studying them today.

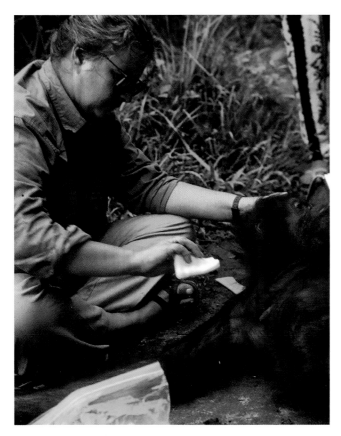

Biruté Galdikas studied orangutans without the use of radio collars, having decided that the risk of injuring or killing one of these endangered animals far outweighed the possible benefits of collaring them.

But along with pursuing scientific knowledge, she has always invested time and effort in caring for individual orangutans. In her field camp, she raises numerous orphaned baby orangutans and pet orangutans and returns them to the wild. Her concern for individual orangutans is also reflected in some of her decisions about her scientific methods.

In 1979, Galdikas had the opportunity to tranquilize and radio collar the orangutans near her field camp. The radio collars would have greatly aided her in her studies. However, for her, the risk of injuring or killing the orangutans was not acceptable. She decided not to capture and radio collar them. Considering these kinds of risks is especially important when working with endangered animals, when only a few are left.

Unwanted Side-Effects

Scientists' efforts to study animals can have unintended effects. Large tags and collars can get caught on trees or slow an animal that's fighting or fleeing. Painting, tagging, or otherwise marking an animal may make other animals treat it differently. For instance, a tagged animal might have more difficulty finding a mate. Or a predator might be able to find it more easily because a colorful tag could give away its location.

Consider, for instance, the scientists who marked the trees where they found raptor nests. They put shiny tin on the trees to mark them. Unfortunately, raccoons figured out that trees with markings had nests. The raccoons went from marked tree to marked tree, gobbling up the birds' eggs. The scientists had to change the mark to protect the nests from predators. For similar reasons, other scientists try to limit how long they spend at birds' nests. They try to avoid activity that could draw a predator's attention to a nest's location. Taking these kinds of precautions safeguards animals. It also ensures a better scientific study, because the study subjects are not killed off by predators and conditions are more similar to natural ones.

CAREFUL CONSIDERATION   Mark and Delia Owens carefully planned their tranquilizing to minimize stress on the animals they were studying. They tranquilized lions at night so the drugged animals would not overheat in the sun. They waited until the lions gathered to feed on a kill before darting them. Already relaxed and crouched down for feeding, the lions were less likely to flee while drugged, and injure themselves.

COSTS AND BENEFITS   Capturing and marking animals undoubtedly has some negative effects on them. At the least, for the first few hours or days after the stress of capture, the animal has less energy for finding food, for mating, and for raising young. Still, the information gained from this work is important to the scientific understanding of animals. And the more people know about animals, their lives, and their needs, the better the chances are that people can help to preserve them and their habitats.

Australian zoologist Frank Carrick uses footprint records to identify koalas that are legally held in captivity.

THE BENEFITS OF KNOWING ANIMALS

Knowing which animal is which is valuable not just for scientific research, but also for conservation. In Australia, it's illegal to capture koalas from the wild. But some people still do, to replace captive koalas that have died. To discourage this practice, zoologist Frank Carrick of the University of Queensland has begun keeping footprint records of koalas that are legally kept in zoos, in tourist parks, and as pets. Koalas can be footprinted, using ink and paper the way human suspects are fingerprinted at police stations. Both people and koalas can later be identified by their prints. By keeping close records of koalas legally in captivity, Carrick hopes to prevent people from secretly replacing captive koalas that die with ones illegally taken from the wild.

4

TOADS WITH BACKPACKS AND EELS ON VIDEO

How Scientists Study Wild Animals' Behavior

To study wild mountain gorillas, Dian Fossey began by quietly observing them. She kept her distance. She watched how the gorillas got along with one another. Then over a period of months, she drew closer to them. To fit in, she even began behaving like a gorilla. She scratched her skin, loudly chewed wild celery stalks, and imitated gorilla calls. Eventually, the gorillas crowded around her, almost as if she was part of the family. Fossey was able to watch the gorillas at close range in order to learn about their behavior.

Following and observing animals at close range is one good way to learn about their behavior. But it's not always practical. For instance, people cannot swim fast enough or long enough to keep up with dolphins. So scientists observe these marine mammals from boat decks, from shorelines, and even from planes. They snorkel, scuba dive, and peer through glass bottom boats to see how dolphins behave. In recent years, scientists have used satellite technologies to track dolphins on long-distance travels. To study other species, scientists use techniques almost as varied as the animals themselves.

GETTING CLOSE TO THEIR SUBJECTS

To study wild primates such as chimpanzees, lemurs, and gorillas, scientists must first get the animals accustomed to their presence. Initially, the animals may run away. But soon, they may become bolder, making threatening displays to try to scare off the people. The chimpanzees Jane Goodall studied sometimes screamed at her, jumped up and down, and shook branches at her in the first year she studied them. Real research can only come much later, when the animals are habituated, meaning they ignore or at least act naturally around the scientist. Then the scientist can follow the animals and record their daily activities.

Getting groups of animals habituated to humans can take many months or even years. Science writer Sy Montgomery, in the preface to *Walking With the Great Apes,* describes how she studied emus. While she was in Australia, studying plants for the Chicago Zoological Society, she became fascinated by emus—giant, flightless birds. So she turned her attention to them instead. Every day she wore the same clothes, and she followed the emus until they were used to her appearance and her behavior. Whether they're studying emus or elephants, field scientists often speak of a kind of "trust" that slowly develops between themselves and the animals they study.

HOW CLOSE IS TOO CLOSE? Field scientists are sometimes criticized for interacting too much with their subjects. Can a person who is acting like a gorilla and sitting in a family group of gorillas really accurately study them? How much does the person's presence change the behavior of the animal family? It is hard to know. But so far, close observation of habituated animals seems to be one of the most practical ways to study wild animals' behavior.

GATHERING DATA ABOUT BEHAVIOR

Field scientists do more than watch animals and scribble random notes. There's a method to what they look for, observe, and record.

NUMBERS COUNT Whenever possible, scientists try to quantify behavior. They don't just write down that the animals ate, played, and bathed. Instead, they may record the durations or frequencies of these activities: 3 hours eating; 2.1 hours playing; 4 baths in one day, and so on. These numbers are useful when scientists compare and contrast different populations, or species, of animals.

THE GREAT HIPPO CHALLENGE

During daylight, hippos aren't hard to find. First, they're big: an adult female weighs two tons (about 2 metric tons). Hippos also tend to gather in rivers, where they wallow in the water and mud in order to regulate their body temperatures. Once you find the hippos, however, it can be hard to study them. They spend most of their time underwater. A scientist on the shore sees little more than grey lumps—the backs of the hippos as they move around. Snorkeling into the water won't help. For one thing, it would be dangerous, because the hippos might charge you. But the main trouble is that the water is muddy. You can't see much anyway!

Despite these problems, biologist Hans Klingel chose to study hippos. He learned to tell the individual hippos apart by the scars that marked their backs and whether they were missing bits of their ears or tails. (Fights with hyenas, other hippos, or brushing against thorny trees probably caused these wounds.)

TAKE A SAMPLING If you watch an animal all day, you cannot accurately write down what it does every second. While you're writing down one thing, the animal is doing another. While you're looking at your paper, you may miss something else! For this reason, and to help quantify behavior, field researchers use a technique called scan sampling. Every five minutes—or some other chosen interval of time—they scan the animal group. They quickly write down what the animals are doing at that particular moment.

FIND A FOCUS Even with scan sampling, recording what's going on can be difficult when working with large groups of animals. That's one reason scientists do focal animal sampling, choosing a focal animal within the group they're watching. They focus on this animal and record its behavior during scan sampling. A premade chart of behaviors allows them to quickly check off behaviors as they occur. A chart might have columns for eating, drinking,

Unfortunately, even these marks can be hard to make out from a distance or difficult to see when a hippo is partly submerged. Klingel tried spraying a small-amount of paint on the hippos hides, to make it easier to identify them. But the paint wore off in a few weeks. So Klingel used a rifle to shoot a dart of anesthetic into some of the hippos. He equipped them with collars and ear tags. These markers helped identify the animals more easily.

Studying hippos at night was still a problem. At night, hippos emerge from rivers, and head into the dense forest and shrublands nearby. Klingel tried following the animals in a jeep, but the going was tough because the vegetation was thick. Apparently, even a big animal such as a hippo can be hard to find at night. Only on moonlit nights could he clearly see the hippos. Some were the ones Klingel had marked with tags or splotches of paint. On dark nights, he and his assistants used flashlights to search for the shine of the hippos' eyes. Through these studies, Klingel learned a lot. But he and other scientists continue to refine techniques for studying these huge animals.

walking, climbing, nursing, grooming, mating, and other behaviors. Scientists may record details such as what is being eaten, and who is being groomed. They may also record nearest neighbors—which animals are nearest their focal animal. This nearness may hint at a special social relationship.

NUMEROUS NOTES   In some studies, several observers may watch an animal group, with each person choosing a different focal animal. In the time between samples, researchers keep a running record of interesting or unusual behaviors. These notes are like a journal or a diary. The sampling fleshes out the picture by giving useful data that can be graphed and charted. This data may reveal trends the observers did not notice at the time.

FOLLOW-THE-LEADER   It's not always possible to physically follow an animal and study its behavior. A wild pig can quickly disappear into a dense for-

This stunning hot-pink rodent has been coated with glow-in-the-dark paint, making it easier to keep track of its movements in the dark.

est. A whale can dive deep into the ocean. A prairie dog can burrow into the ground. As a result, some scientists must try unusual techniques to track animals' on their travels.

In a forest in Madagascar, a scientist wanted to find out where native rats travel during the night. So she tied a thin thread to one rat's tail and let the thread unroll from a spool. By the next morning, nearby trees were interwoven with the thread, clearly showing the rat's path, here, there, and everywhere! Meanwhile, in the Florida Keys, biologist Numi Goodyear, who was also studying rats, chose a different tracking technique. She dusted rats with powdered, glow-in-the-dark paint. Wherever the rats traveled, they left behind a sprinkling of the bright paint!

FROM SIGNALS TO SATELLITES: NEW TECHNOLOGIES

Imagine being in a cave, underwater, at night, and looking for one of the slimiest creatures on Earth. That's what Dr. Gene S. Helfman, associate professor at the University of Georgia, does when he's studying eels. Eels are slime-covered, snakelike fish. Helfman studies their behavior by scuba diving down into water-filled caves in Florida. But he can't watch the eels every hour of the day. The water's cold, and people cannot scuba dive for very long. So Helfman sets up a video camera to film the animals' behavior when he's not there. Video is only one of the many kinds of technology that is revolutionizing the study of wild animals. Today field scientists are assisted by radio transmitters, radio receivers, computers, and even satellites.

FOLLOW THE BEEPS Radio tracking is a popular method for following animals on their daily routes. First, the scientist attaches a transmitter to the animal. The transmitter emits radio signals. The scientist holds a receiver that hears the signal and registers it as a series of beeps. The closer the animal is, the closer together the beeps will sound. The farther away it is, the more time between beeps. Attached to the scientist's receiver is a large antenna that helps improve reception of the signal.

To find an animal, scientists can walk, drive, or ski back and forth, following the beeps. But typically, they use a method called triangulation, to more rapidly determine the animal's location. First, they move to the highest spot in the area—usually a hill. They turn the antenna slowly until it is pointing toward the strongest signal. Using a compass, they determine in what direction the antenna is pointing. Then they mark it down on a map, drawing a line from their location toward the place where the strongest signal readings are coming from. Next, the scientists walk or drive to another high point and repeat the process, locating the signal again. Now their map contains two lines. Wherever these lines cross is the animal's approximate location. They can move to that area to find the animal. (Of course, there's always the problem that the animal may have run a long way since the readings were made!) Hills, radio towers, and other objects can also interfere with radio signals and throw off triangulation calculations.

Radio tracking makes it possible to follow specific animals as they go about their daily routines.

Here a yearling bear is returned to its den after being fitted with a radio collar.

Radio tracking has been used to follow the movements of caribou, wolves, possums, dolphins, eels, and even dung beetles. Recently, scientists radio collared a fox and tracked its nighttime travels through the streets and alleys of Washington, D.C.! Radio tracking has been very useful for determining how far and how fast animals travel in a day. By following animals' daily and seasonal movements, biologists have gotten a better idea of how much room animals need. These measurements are important in planning the dimensions of parks and refuges for endangered animals.

IMPROVING TECHNOLOGY   Early radio transmitters were large, bulky devices. They were attached to animals by collars. By radio collaring animals, Delia and Mark Owens were able to track jackals, lions, and brown hyenas across the Kalahari. But in recent years, miniature devices have revolutionized the field. Some transmitters are so small they can be implanted underneath a snake's skin or glued to the back of a beetle.

Originally, radio tracking devices only told scientists where the animals were. But today, special tracking devices can monitor animals' heart rates, temperatures, and even the depths to which they dive and how fast they swim. An elephant seal was recently tracked diving 5,000 feet (1,524 meters)— almost a mile (1.5 kilometers) deep!

Even with these advances in technology, radio collaring some animals can still be a challenge. Toads, which have fragile skin and no real neck, can't be easily collared or injected with a transmitter. Gluing on a transmitter won't work either, because poisonous chemicals in the glue can seep through the toad's moist skin. So when Bob Johnson, curator of amphibians at the Metropolitan Toronto Zoo, wanted to track toads, he had to come up with his own tracking technique.

First, he designed a mesh fabric harness that would hold transmitters on the toads. But that didn't work. The toads, perhaps alarmed by the strange outfits, puffed up with air until the mesh material popped off! After that discouraging result, Johnson took the unusual step of enlisting the help of two fashion designers in Toronto. (Normally the two designers, Joyce Gunhouse and Judy Cornish, design clothes for people, not toads.) But they were game for this project. Using girdle material, they designed a waterproof, flexible backpack that could be fastened on by straps around a toad's waist and under its jaws. The backpacks may not have been a fashion success, but they were definitely a scientific one. The backpacks with transmitters were used by Johnson to track captive-bred Puerto Rican crested toads he released into the wild.

WHERE IN THE WORLD?   One of the big changes in the study of wild animals is the use of satellite technology. By sending signals to satellites and receiving signals back, a scientist can find out almost exactly where he or she is on earth. A small, handheld, global positioning device does the job, giving readings in terms of latitude and longitude. This allows scientists to accurately record the location of animals, nests, burrows, and the like. The technology also has great potential for use in tracking animals. Already, it has been used to track Asian elephants. Zoologist Michael Stuewe of the National Zoo's Conservation and Research Center in Front Royal, Virginia, attached a transmitter to the collar of an elephant in Malaysia. The collar transmitted signals to satellites, which monitored its position.

CANDID CAMERAS AND COMPUTERS   Laptop computers are widely used in tracking animals today. Laptop computers record and graph data, on-site, in the field. With computers on site, scientists can analyze data immediately and make any needed changes in their study techniques.

CHEMICAL TRAILS   Advances in the field of chemistry are also helping scientists track animals. For instance, tracking monarch butterflies with paper

Monarch butterflies migrate south for the winter. The butterflies in this photograph, taken in Mexico, may have come from the northern United States or Canada.

tags may soon be supplemented by a special kind of chemical tracking. Scientists hope to be able to capture a butterfly and run chemical tests on its cells to find out in what region of the country it was raised. The idea is based, strangely enough, on differences in rainwater.

Rainwater is made up of hydrogen and oxygen. But there are two types of hydrogen: regular hydrogen and deuterium, also known as heavy hydrogen. Some deuterium occurs naturally in rainwater. How much varies from region to region in North America.

How does deuterium help scientists who are studying butterflies? The rain, which contains deuterium, is absorbed by the roots of the milkweed plants that monarch caterpillars eat. So some of the deuterium in the rain is passed along to the caterpillars, and ultimately, the butterflies. By analyzing the percentage of deuterium in a monarch butterfly's body, scientists may one day be able to figure out what part of the country it came from.

WILDLIFE STUDY IN A MODERN AGE

These days, field biologists use a wide range of techniques to follow and study animals. They follow animals on foot, fly airplanes to pursue dolphins, and drive boats to chase whales. They videotape monkeys and radiotrack elephants. Satellites, lasers, radio transmitters, and chemical technologies may make research easier. But funds for studying animals are limited, so only a few scientists can take advantage of such high-tech equipment. Despite all the new technologies, careful observation and determination remain the field scientist's most frequently used tools.

5

HYENAS IN THE KITCHEN, MAMBAS ON THE ROOF

The Life and Career of a Field Scientist

If you're a scientist in a desert or rain forest, one of the first things you learn is that scorpions tend to crawl into dark corners, like the toes of boots. So you should always shake out your boots before you put them on. You may also want to shine a flashlight into your sleeping bag, just in case of snakes. And last but not least, don't leave food in your tent. You don't want a monkey to rip up your bags, seeking food. Such things happen. Scientists have even been known to find mambas—poisonous snakes—on their field camp's roof!

These conditions, which scientists face in the field, may sound dramatic and difficult. But many scientists find handling other aspects of their careers equally challenging. In addition to studying animals, a scientist may need to track down funding, fill out paperwork, manage field assistants, write scientific papers, teach classes, work with colleagues, negotiate with government agencies, and handle a mind-boggling variety of other tasks. What they do depends on their educational training, study site, and overall career.

EMPLOYMENT OPPORTUNITIES

Scientists who study animals in the wild don't all have the same sort of jobs. The reasons for their work, the conditions under which they work, and the funding of their work vary considerably.

ACADEMIC OPTIONS   Many field scientists are professors of biology, zoology, anthropology, or environmental studies at a college or university. They carry out their field research in between classes, during vacations, or during semesters when they do not teach. Their undergraduate and graduate students may assist them with their field research.

GOVERNMENT JOBS   Other field scientists work for the government in state wildlife agencies, the National Park Service, the Fish and Wildlife Service, the Forest Service, or the Bureau of Land Management. Their research may be used in managing public lands such as national parks, national forests, and national wildlife refuges. Some of these biologists work on programs to help endangered species such as manatees, Florida panthers, and red-cockaded woodpeckers. Other duties can include managing hunting, fishing, and trapping, and teaching the public about nature.

The National Park Service employs a large number of field scientists. Here a park ranger gives a lecture about the slug she's holding in her hand.

PRIVATELY EMPLOYED   In some cases, field scientists work on staff for conservation groups. Or they work for environmental consulting firms, which do contract work for private business or the government. For instance, a scientist at a consulting firm may survey an area to make sure no endangered species live there before an airport or mall is built.

More About the Real Moose Man

The title of this book was inspired by a real scientist, Dr. Anthony Bubenik. He was an eminent field biologist who wore a moose head, complete with antlers, and walked into areas that moose frequented. He would wear big boots and step heavily, putting his weight first on his toes, then on his heels. This made a two-beat clomping sound like a moose's hooves. Using this technique, Bubenik attracted both male and female moose.

Alaskan bull moose

Bubenik was interested in the role antlers play in the interactions between moose. He also studied how antlers affect the behavior of other members of the deer family, such as deer and caribou. The dummy moose head and antlers Bubenik wore helped him test moose's reactions to other moose's antlers. For instance, he found that moose and other deer communicate by the way they turn their heads and angle their antlers. Turn antlers one way, and it's a challenge to battle. Turn antlers another way, showing off their size, and it may indicate a moose's strength. Turn antlers still another way, and it could mean a moose is backing down from a fight.

A strange aspect of Bubenik's moose experiments is that the moose reacted to him as if he were another moose. True, in front, he looked like a moose, because he was wearing the moose head and antlers. And in the back, his costume was a little like a moose's rump. But wild moose didn't seem to notice that this "moose" had only two legs instead of four! Bubenik's fake front and fake rump

GRANT-FUNDED RESEARCH   A few field researchers rely entirely on grant money to support themselves. The National Geographic Society, the World Wildlife Fund, and various private foundations donate money to support researchers. However, the funds for such work are not plentiful. Often, field scientists must scrimp and save to cover their research costs and must fund some of their research with their own money.

were enough to stimulate the moose's natural behaviors. It did not seem to matter that there was no long, mooselike body in between!

Despite all his potentially dangerous encounters with moose and deer, Bubenik was seriously injured only once. A captive Wapiti deer knocked him to the ground, injuring his spine. He spent a year in bed, immobilized, in traction.

Bubenik's career had an unusual start and some major twists and turns. He was born in 1913 in Moravia, a country that later became part of Czechoslovakia and today is in the Czech Republic. He started not in biology, but in chemistry. He earned a Ph.D. in organic chemistry. Then he started teaching at a university. But he lost his teaching job when the Nazis closed the university.

After World War II, Bubenik decided to abandon chemistry and go into biology. He was very successful studying deer. Eventually, he was made director of Wildlife Research at the Czech Academy of the Sciences. But politics got in the way of his career once again. Bubenik refused to join the Communist Party, the party in power. As a result, in 1958 he lost his job and was sentenced to manual labor for life. Fortunately, his sentence was terminated in 1965 and he was able to move to Yugoslavia. He and his family later moved to Switzerland, then finally to Canada.

In Canada, Bubenik worked as a biologist for the Ontario Ministry of Natural Resources. He was very active in his field, writing books and hundreds of articles for scientific journals and for magazines. Able to speak seven languages, Bubenik traveled extensively, consulting with scientists worldwide about deer. He also loved to hunt, draw animals, film wildlife, raise orchids, and spend time with his family. Dr. Bubenik died peacefully, while out walking his dog, in February 1995.

EDUCATIONAL REQUIREMENTS

The educational background of field scientists varies. But in general, field scientists have bachelor's degrees in science (B.S.) from a four-year university. They major in wildlife biology, ecology, zoology, environmental studies, or some other related field. Primatologists, who study primates such as monkeys and apes, often have degrees in anthropology instead. That's because anthropology is the social science that deals with humans. Humans are primates, and much of the study of other primates began as a way to understand the behavior of humans or their prehuman ancestors.

With a B.S., many graduates go on to get internships or short-term, low-paying jobs. Usually, these are jobs working on field studies under another scientist's supervision. Eventually, most career field scientists go on to get a master's degree in science (M.S.) or a doctoral degree (Ph.D.). The master's degree and Ph.D. can be in zoology, wildlife biology, ecology, evolutionary biology, primatology, or other scientific fields. A master's degree is generally sufficient to work on staff for the government, conservation groups, or environmental consulting firms. But to get a permanent position as a university professor, a scientist needs a Ph.D.

Full-time, permanent jobs are few and far between. Most field scientists start their careers as interns or graduate students. They work under the supervision of other scientists before they move on to manage their own projects.

People don't go into the profession of field science for the money. Jobs are relatively low-paying, considering the educational background required. Yet despite the difficulties of this kind of career, most field scientists, when asked, say they wouldn't switch their career for any other one. The thrill of discovering a new species, the satisfaction of adding another piece of information to the body of scientific knowledge, the joy of working with wild animals, and spending time in nature are just a few of the rewarding aspects of a career in field science.

WHO CAN BE A FIELD BIOLOGIST?

You don't have to be a big, muscular, tiger-wrestling man to be a field scientist. Men and women of many races, nationalities, and body types are field biologists. People with physical challenges, such as asthma, deafness, or blindness, have gone on to do successful work studying animals, too.

WOMEN AT WORK In the early years of field science, not many women carried out formal field studies of animals. But these days, female scientists study everything from anacondas to sharks. Their work in primatology has been particularly successful. Research done by women has overturned many mistaken beliefs about the structure of primate societies in the wild. Some primate societies, once thought to be dominated by the male primates, turn out to be dominated by the females, after all!

GLOBAL SCIENTISTS Europeans, Canadians, and Americans did much of the early work in field science, even in other parts of the world. But renowned researchers now come from many countries, from Madagascar to Malaysia. Europeans, Canadians, and Americans who set up research projects in other countries frequently train local people in research techniques. Local people often have the advantage of decades of on-site learning about the animals and plants around them. These homegrown scientists can go on to get research degrees in their native countries or elsewhere in the world. Then they may continue or expand on their previous fieldwork.

OVERCOMING HEALTH CHALLENGES Being a field scientist doesn't mean you have to travel to exotic countries or live in a tent. There are plenty of animals to study close to home. For some studies, you can go out and do research and return home that very night. Other research projects, in remote areas, may pose physical challenges. Field studies may require coping with blistering heat, long, cold hikes, or biting insects, or living in field camps for long periods.

Being very healthy to start with helps a lot. But some field scientists endure difficult conditions while managing health concerns and physical challenges. Dian Fossey, the famous primatologist, had asthma. At times, she struggled to hike up and down the hills where she studied gorillas.

Another renowned field scientist, Dr. Geerat Vermeij, travels the globe, gathering sea snails from tide pools and other shallow waters. His blindness has not prevented him from becoming one of the world's experts on sea snail shells. Vermeij, a professor of geology at the University of California at Davis, is the recipient of a MacArthur "genius" fellowship. He studies the shapes, patterns, and textures of the snail shells entirely with his fingers and his mind. By examining a snail shell with his fingers, he can tell if it has ever been attacked by a predator. If it has been attacked, the shell is thicker where the shell has regrown to repair damage caused by the predator. In his studies of shells, Vermeij has noticed many peculiarities his sighted colleagues have not. Using this information, he's made major discoveries about evolution.

A PATH TO A REWARDING CAREER

You don't have to take a conventional path to end up in a job studying animals. Patricia Wright's career is a case in point. Wright had always been interested in animals and had studied biology in college. But after college, she became a social worker in New York City. She got married, and had a child.

local language and being on good terms with local people and governments helps foreign field scientists minimize such dangers. Conditions vary tremendously from country to country.

Another problem with long-term foreign fieldwork is the strain it can put on scientists' families. Marriages and other relationships can suffer from long periods of separation when scientists are in the field. Some couples have been able to combine their talents to make a strong research team. Mark and Delia Owens studied lions, jackals, and brown hyenas in Africa. Peter and Mary Grant studied finches in the Galápagos Islands. In a few cases, scientists have brought their spouses and children with them into the field, to live in their research camps. Other scientists do their fieldwork for a few months, then return home for a few months, then go back into the field, and so on, throughout the year.

Overall, the risks associated with foreign fieldwork have more to do with being away from home and traveling than with the work. On the positive side, traveling and learning about other people's cultures and building friendships across the world bring their own rewards. The things most people fear about fieldwork—the snakes, tigers, lions, spiders, and so on—often turn out to be less problematic than expected.

Few people at that time would have guessed she'd become a world-renowned primatologist.

While Wright was at home raising her daughter, her pet monkeys were raising a baby of their own. Watching the monkeys made Wright curious about how wild primates take care of their young. Inspired, she returned to school to get her Ph.D. in anthropology. She and her young daughter even spent months living in a tent in a South American rain forest while Wright studied monkeys in the wild.

When I met Dr. Wright, she was teaching at Duke University and studying lemurs. Wright seemed dynamic, brilliant, strong-minded, and a little bit eccentric—just the kind of professor I liked. When she recognized my interest in primatology, she asked me to work with her at the Duke Primate Center. There, I sat in the lemur's cages, watching their behavior, and recording it for her studies. I even had the privilege of watching and monitoring a baby tarsier—the first born in captivity in the United States.

Sometimes, Wright and I would discuss her latest theories about the primates she was studying. Her curiosity about animal behavior, her passion for scientific discovery, and her pure joy in learning inspired me and many other students to follow in her footsteps. Somehow, she made sitting in the cage of a smelly primate, hour after hour, in the hot summer, under red lamps, with crickets crawling over us, seem like the most exciting scientific adventure in the world.

Today, Dr. Wright not only studies lemurs, but also teaches at the State University of New York at Stony Brook and helps coordinate conservation efforts in Madagascar. In 1990, my husband and I traveled to her field camp in Madagascar to study lemurs with her. Before dawn, we'd crawl out of our tents and grab some breakfast. Then, with the guidance of local men Wright had trained, we'd hike out to where the lemurs were sleeping. Once the lemurs woke, we'd spend the day following their every movement until they went to sleep. At times, following them was a tremendous challenge. They'd leap, seemingly effortlessly, from tree to tree. Meanwhile, we humans would run along the ground, tear through tangled vines, climb slippery slopes, leap over fallen trees, and wade through streams, trying to keep the lemurs in sight. Our observations of the lemurs became part of Wright's long-term study of the behavior of these lemur family groups.

At the research camp, scientists and graduate students from many countries worked to study animals and plants. Wright worked there, too. But she spent much of her time doing other, nonscientific tasks. When she wasn't out negotiating with government officials, she was coordinating local efforts at conservation. Or she was talking with *Wall Street Journal* reporters who had come to visit. Or she was setting up a museum for local children in town. Or she was off on an expedition to an unexplored area. Dr. Wright admits hers is a busy life:

"I don't notice the long hours . . . I'm so busy and interested by my work," she says. "But sometimes, of course, I do get exhausted. The other night I was really exhausted . . . I was just *so* busy, and I started thinking about what I needed to do . . . Then, suddenly, I realized: You know, this is the greatest job in the world! I'm really perfectly happy even though I'm busy. I really like my job."

Wright's love of her job is evident. Whenever we did manage to catch up with Wright, her enthusiasm for scientific study was infectious. We'd tramp around the forest, studying anything we found—from lemurs to snails to butterflies. Frequently, she'd pull a notebook out of one of the pockets in her green vest and scribble a few things down. Once, she tried to talk me into studying leeches.

"We really need someone to study leeches!" she said, beaming, as if it were the most delightful job in the world. I was content to flick the leeches off my legs and not ever see the little creatures again.

This is the giant earthworm Dr. Patricia Wright pulled out of her pocket!

In the rain forest in Madagascar, we often found new animals, creatures none of us had seen before. When we did, we'd bring them back to camp to be photographed and examined more closely by scientific experts. One night, after we had all been sitting at dinner for about an hour, Wright said, "Oh! I almost forgot! Look what I found on the trail!"

Out of her pants pocket she pulled a truly gigantic earthworm: about two feet (61 centimeters) long, thicker than a thumb, and still alive. Her face was glowing with the same kind of joy you might see on a kid who had just found a neat frog in a pond. That kind of pleasure in new discoveries is just one of the many reasons Patricia Wright and other field scientists love their jobs so much.

To those who want to follow in her footsteps, Wright advises, "The bottom line is to figure out what you want to do, and then do it the best you can. If you're interested in studying animals, everybody will tell you there are no jobs studying animals. But if you are really dedicated, and you do a good job of it, there's always a job out there for you."

To find out how *you* can get a head start on a career in field science by getting experience working with animals, read the next section, "You Can Get Involved in Animal Studies."

You Can Get Involved in Animal Studies

You don't have to wait until you're in college to study animals. Students in elementary, middle, and high school often get involved, too. Here are some organizations to contact if you're interested in helping with field studies of animals:

- *Local chapter of the Audubon Society* Yearly bird counts, one in December and one in May, are carried out by local chapters of the Audubon Society. They sometimes have butterfly counts, too. They also may carry out surveys of nesting birds in summer. Some Audubon members set up banding stations, for banding birds.

- *Monarch Watch* Each year, parents, teachers, and students participate in Monarch Watch, a program to capture, tag, and release monarch butterflies. For information on how you can participate, check the Monarch Watch World Wide Web page at: **http://monarch.bio.ukans.edu**

  This web page contains extensive information on monarchs, maps of tagging sites across the United States and Canada, plus information on how you can get a tagging kit. You may also request a tagging kit by e-mail at: **monarch@falcon.cc.ukans.edu**

  Or, you can write and order one from:

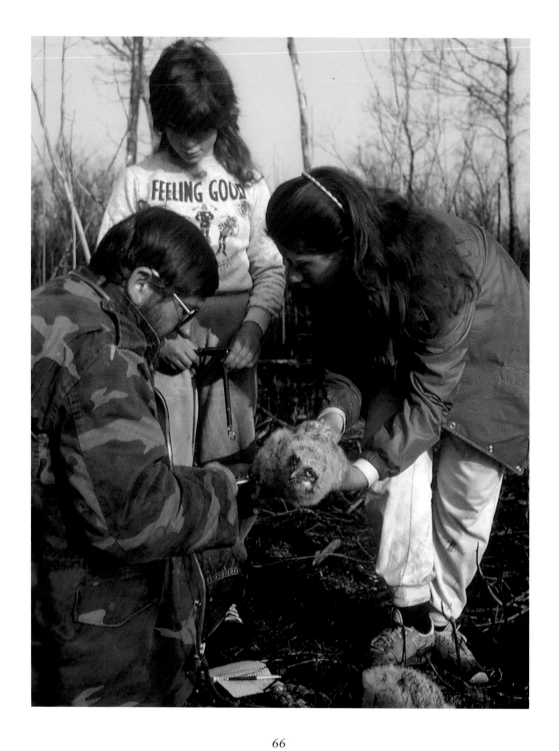

66

Monarch Watch
O.R. "Chip" Taylor
Department of Entomology
University of Kansas, Haworth Hall
Lawrence, KS 66045-2106

- *Nature Centers*   They often have scientific studies that students can help with. Nature centers may survey frogs, birds, or deer on their property. Or they may offer programs about animal tracking that would help you polish your animal study skills. If they don't have a special program, ask about setting up your own study with their help.

- *National Parks, State Parks, National Wildlife Refuges, National Forests* If you live near parks, refuges, or national forests, contact the rangers or naturalists there to see if they need help with any field research on animals.

- *State Departments of Wildlife or Natural Resources*   By calling the offices of these state agencies, you may be able to find out about wildlife studies in your area.

- *University or College Biology Departments*   If you express a special interest in field research, a professor or graduate student might let you accompany them and help them with a field study.

- *Zoos and Raptor Rehabilitation Centers*   Zoos and raptor rehabilitation centers—places that help hawks, owls, and eagles recover from injuries—primarily work with animals in captivity. But by volunteering at these places, you can learn more about animals. You might be able to be a docent—someone who teaches the public about the animals in the zoo or rehab center. Or the staff may know about field studies of wild animals that you could participate in.

If you cannot find anyone doing animal studies in your area, don't give up. Check out field guides and animal books from your library. Spend as much time as you can in parks or natural areas, observing animals. Some of the best naturalists and scientists began by teaching themselves nature skills.

Glossary

census—a count, or tally, of a population

data—factual information that scientists gather

English system—the system of measurement that uses feet, pounds, and inches

field marks—the characteristics of animals that can be used to identify them in the wild under field conditions, as opposed to laboratory conditions

field scientist—a scientist who carries out research outdoors, not just in the laboratory

focal animal—an animal a scientist chooses to concentrate on when studying behavior

genetic material—the molecules that determine the physical characteristics of an organism

global positioning device—a machine that can determine position on earth by sending a signal to a network of satellites and receiving signals back

habituate—the process by which animals become accustomed to the presence of human observers

metric system—an international system of measurement that uses meters, kilograms, and hectares

primate—mammals such as apes, monkeys, lemurs, and humans

radio tracking—following the path an animal takes by receiving and analyzing radio signals sent by a transmitter that is attached to the animal

scan sampling—a method of analyzing animal behavior by glancing at an animal or a group of animals periodically and recording what they are doing

scat—animal droppings or feces

scientific name—term used by scientists to describe an organism

specimen—a sample item or organism collected by a scientist for study

tranquilizer—a drug that makes an animal groggy or unconscious

triangulation—a method for finding the position of something by measuring two bearings a known distance apart

FURTHER READING

For more information on the scientists, animals, and research techniques mentioned in this book, look at the following books:

Animal Behavior Science Projects by Nancy Woodward Cain (John Wiley & Sons, 1995).

Batman: Exploring the World of Bats by Laurence Pringle (Scribners, 1983).

Bearman: Exploring the World of Black Bears by Laurence Pringle (Scribners, 1991).

Dolphin Man: Exploring the World of Dolphins by Laurence Pringle (Atheneum, 1995).

Echo of the Elephants: The Story of an Elephant Family by Cynthia Moss (William Morrow and Company, 1992).

The Encyclopedia of Animal Behavior edited by Peter J.B. Slater (Facts on File, 1987).

A Guide to Animal Tracking and Behavior by Donald Stokes and Lillian Stokes (Little, Brown, and Company, 1986).

Jackal Woman: Exploring the World of Jackals by Laurence Pringle (Scribners, 1993).

Tom Brown's Field Guide to Nature Observation and Tracking by Tom Brown Jr. with Brandt Morgan (Berkeley Books, 1983).

Wildlife Rescue: The Work of Dr. Kathleen Ramsay by Jennifer Dewey (Boyds Mills Press, 1994).

Wolfman: Exploring the World of Wolves by Laurence Pringle (Scribners, 1983).

OTHER RESOURCES

VIDEO

Check your public library, school library, or video store for nature videos. Nature documentaries about animals often include interviews with scientists. National Geographic, NOVA, and Audubon videos are some of the most likely to include interviews with scientists. The following videos feature scientists mentioned in this book:

Among the Wild Chimpanzees (A video about Jane Goodall), National Geographic Society, 1994.

People of the Forest: The Chimps of Gombe (A video about the chimpanzees Jane Goodall studied), The Discovery Channel, 1991.

Search for the Great Apes (A video about Dian Fossey and Biruté Galdikas), National Geographic Society, 1975.

WORLD WIDE WEB

A large number of World Wide Web pages cover science and scientists. However, these addresses change rapidly, so only a few key sites are listed here. The best way to find relevant World Wide Web sites is to look under "science" headings on your home screen. Or use a search engine to look for information about a specific type of animal. Here are a few sites to get you started:

Animal Links

http://www.mindspring.com/~zoonet/anilinks.html

This site can connect you with many different web pages about animals.

Facts about Federal Wildlife Laws

http://www/fws.gov/~pullenl/wildlaw/wildlaws.html

Produced by the U.S. Fish and Wildlife Service, this site lists and explains laws that affect the export, import, capture, and handling of wild animals.

Vose School Education Resources

http://www.teleport.com/~vincer/starter.html

This site helps link students and teachers to web pages and has a section that links to Science Resources elsewhere on the web.

Sources

GENERAL

Halfpenny, James. *Field Guide to Mammal Tracking in North America.* Boulder, Col.: Johnson Books, 1986.

Johnson, Donna. "How to Tag a Bevy of Bees," *National Wildlife,* February/March 1993, 24–27.

Turbak, Gary. "The Great American Wildlife Census," *National Wildlife,* April/May 1990, 34–37.

MAMMALS

Barnes, Richard, and Karen Barnes. "You Can't See the Elephants for the Trees," *Wildlife Conservation,* March/April 1990, 39–45.

Galdikas, Biruté M. F. *Reflections of Eden: My Years With the Orangutans of Borneo.* Boston: Little, Brown, and Company, Inc., 1995.

Klingel, Hans. "Fluctuating Fortunes of the River Horse" (hippos), *Natural History,* May 1995, 46–56.

McAuliffe, Kathleen. "Elephant Seals, the Champion Divers of the Deep," *Smithsonian,* September 1995, 44–46.

Montgomery, Sy. *Walking with the Great Apes.* Boston: Houghton Mifflin, 1991.

Norris, Kenneth S. *The Life and Times of the Spinner Dolphin.* New York: Avon, 1993.

Owens, Mark J. and Delia D. Owens. *Cry of the Kalahari*. Boston: Houghton Mifflin, 1984.

Parfit, Michael. "Its Days as a Varmint Are Over, but the Cougar Is Still on the Run," *Smithsonian*, September 1995, 68–79.

Poole, Joyce. *Coming of Age with Elephants: A Memoir*. New York: Hyperion, 1996.

Quigley, Howard, and Maurice Hornocker. "On the Trail of Russia's Leopards," *International Wildlife*, May/June 1995, 38–43.

Seidensticker, John, with Susan Lumpkin. "Playing Possum Is Serious Business for Our Only Marsupial," *Smithsonian*, November 1989, 109–122.

BIRDS

Jaffe, Mark. *And No Birds Sing*. New York: Simon and Schuster, 1994.

Katz, Barbara. *So Cranes May Dance*. Chicago: Chicago Review Press, 1993.

Stap, Don. *A Parrot Without a Name: The Search for the Last Known Birds on Earth*. New York: Knopf, 1990.

Weiner, Jonathan. *The Beak of the Finch*. New York: Knopf, 1994.

REPTILES AND AMPHIBIANS

Kemper, Steve. "If It Moves, Grab It, but Try Not to Get the End That Bites" (anacondas), *Smithsonian*, September 1996, 43–51.

Kingsmill, Suzanne. "How to Track a Toad," *International Wildlife*, January/February 1991, 29.

Wexler, Mark. "Modern Mission to Save an Ancient Mariner" (sea turtles), *National Wildlife*, June/July 1988, 4–11.

FISH

Helfman, Gene S. "Spinning for Their Supper" (eels), *Natural History*, May 1995, 26–29.

Klimley, A. Peter. "Hammerhead City" (sharks), *Natural History*, October 1995, 33–39.

INSECTS AND OTHER INVERTEBRATES

Connisf, Richard. "Clyde Roper Can't Wait To Be Attacked by the Giant Squid," *Smithsonian*, May 1996, 126–136.

Dethier, Vincent G. *Crickets and Katydids, Concerts and Solos.* Cambridge, Mass.: Harvard University Press, 1992.

Matthews, Downs. "Mountain Monarchs," *Wildlife Conservation,* September/October 1992, 27–29 and 78.

Pyle, Robert Michael. *Handbook for Butterfly Watchers.* Boston: Houghton Mifflin, 1992.

Ross, Gary Noel. "Butterfly Wrangling in Louisiana," *Natural History,* May 1995, 36–42.

Ross, John F. "In the Company of Cannibals That Sting . . . and Glow" (scorpions), *Smithsonian,* April 1996, 92–102.

Ryan, Michael. "He Feels the Shape of the Past" (Dr. Vermeij, molluscs), *Parade,* July 7, 1996, 14–15.

Wilson, E. O. *Naturalist* (ants). Washington, D.C.: Island Press, 1994.

INDEX

References to illustrations are listed in *italic, **boldface*** type.

Photo Credits